Procrastination is the Assignation of Motivation

BY

DAVID MICHAEL PENA

With

Ms. Jitra Sauvnmit

DETICATION

TO CREATESPACE.COM FOR
PUBLISHING AND WEERACHON
KOSENANST FOR EDITING

INTRODUCTION

Now those of you have you that have read any of my book sometimes I get very passionate and you adult language so if this off offends you please close this book now and go phone your mommy. If not then let's begin. Now what is motivation and what is procrastination? Motivation comes from two sources: oneself, and other people. These two sources are called intrinsic motivation and extrinsic motivation, respectively Negative reinforcement involves stimulus change consisting of the removal of an aversive stimulus following a response. Positive reinforcement involves a stimulus change consisting of the presentation or magnification of a positive stimulus following a response.

From this perspective, motivation is mediated by environmental events, and the concept of distinguishing between intrinsic and extrinsic forces is irrelevant.

Negative reinforcement involves stimulus change consisting of the removal of an aversive stimulus following a response. Positive reinforcement involves a stimulus change consisting of the presentation or magnification of a positive stimulus following a response. From this perspective, motivation is mediated by environmental events, and the concept of distinguishing between intrinsic and extrinsic forces is irrelevant. Now studies by David McClelland have shown that money is a poor motivator. And I couldn't agree with him more. If money motivates us we would work 16 hours a day and 7 days a week. Wouldn't we if money truly motivated us? If we want money so much then why don't we do the things necessary for making at much as possible. Right? **Why we do is get enthusiastic about a new goal, start working hard and then completely burn ourselves out a week later? This is why companies have contests and awards** because it's a proven fact the human being works harder to achieve or win a contest or award of some sort. Now we all like money don't get me wrong, and let's face it, they say money can't buy happiness, but when I can take my spouse to the movies and shopping at the mall we buy ourselves a lot of happiness. But you see when we focus on our goals instead of money when we hit your goals the money follows right behind, because the money is just not enough. Money will motivate us for only a short period of time and then we lose our focus. So most of our companies we work for have a trips or some kind of tangible prize we can earn by hitting a certain quota, thus giving us more incentive to work harder for the company. Now I recommend shooting for a contest or prize and in turn if you hit you goals, the money will come along side. Now we need to focus on the bigger picture, but most of the time we want instant gratification. We want everything now and don't keep our eyes on the picture. This is why we must have that reason why? Why are we out here at 10:00PM? Why I am in the office on a Sunday making sales calls?

Because when we focused on that trip or tangible prize, we stay focused on our monthly goals. This will help us stay motivated

Now different individuals tend to be motivated by different

factors at different times. It was introduced in a 2006 Academy of Management Review article, in a single formulation the primary aspects of several other major motivational theories, including Incentive Theory, Drive Theory, Need Theory, Self-Efficacy and Goal

Setting. It simplifies the field of motivation and allows findings from one theory to be translated into terms of another

Achievement Motivation

Achievement motivation is an integrative

perspective based on the premise that performance motivation results from the way of broad components of personality are directed towards ones performance. As a result, it includes a range of dimensions that are relevant to success at work

Volition Motivation

This seen as the process that leads to the forming of behavioural intentions. Volition is seen as a process that leads from intention to actual behaviour. In other words, motivation and volition refer to goal setting and goal pursuit, respectively.

Performance Motivation

Performance motivation is a result by way of broad components of personality and are directed to achievement motivation which is an integrative perspective based on the premise that allows us to perform. As a result, it includes a range of dimensions that are relevant to success at work but which are not conventionally regarded as being part of performance motivation

The Now in the early 1950's David C. McClelland and John W.

Atkinson suggested the Achievement Motivation Inventory Theory, which is based on the theory that assesses three factors relevant to vocational and professional success. This motivation has repeatedly been linked with adaptive motivational patterns, including working hard, a willingness to pick learning tasks with much difficulty, and contributing our successes to our efforts. These are the 3 Components in his theory:

1. People would prefer a work environment in which they are able to assume

responsibility for solving problems.

2. People would take calculated RISK and establish moderate, attainable goals.

3. People want to hear continuous recognition, as well as feedback, in order for them to know how well they are doing.

The job characteristics Model (JCM), as designed by Hackman and Oldham attempts to use job design to improve employee motivation. They show that any job can be described in terms of five key job characteristics:

1. **Skill Variety** - the degree to which the job requires the use of different skills and talents

2. **Task Identity** - the degree to which the job has contributed to a clearly identifiable larger project

3. **Task Significance** - the degree to which

the job has an impact on the lives or work of other people

4. Autonomy - the degree to which the employee has independence, freedom and discretion in carrying out the job

5. Task Feedback - the degree to which the employee is

provided with clear, specific, detailed, actionable information about the effectiveness of his or her job performance. This suggest his theory:

$$MPS = \frac{\text{Skill Variety} + \text{Task Identity} + \text{Task Significance}}{3} \times \text{Autonomy} \times \text{Feedback}$$

Now comes the word Procrastination. What is the definition of this word? Procrastination is carrying out less urgent tasks in preference to more urgent ones, or doing more pleasurable things, like taking off early to go out drinking with our piers, in place of less pleasurable ones, like making that's late sales call, knocking that last door, or finishing that spread sheet late at night so it ready for presentation in the morning and thus putting off impending tasks to a later time, sometimes to the "last minute" before the a deadline. Now in the world of selling we tend to us the terms, "we'll call it a day and get a fresh start tomorrow. When we put of doing things until tomorrow, that tomorrow never comes and we don't hit goals, thus this kills our motivation.

Procrastination may result in stress. Individuals coping with responses to procrastination are often emotional or avoidant oriented rather than task or problem-solving oriented.

Emotion oriented coping is designed to reduce stress, associated with putting off intended and important personal goals, an option that provides immediate pleasure and is consequently very attractive to impulsive procrastinators. When we procrastinate we tend to have a feeling or sense of guilt and severe loss of personal productivity. Steel's theory explained in 2001, "actions must be postponed and this postponement will result in poor, inadequate, or inefficient planning. Procrastination can be persistent and tremendously disruptive one in everyday life. If we put off making that sales call or knocking that door at 9:00 PM at night, then most of the time we are losing the customers that we generally want to have. You see what I have learned is the customers that are more qualified to purchase high ticket items are the ones we can only catch in the late evening and weekends. Now if you a sales person and you are not working the nights and weekends, you're missing the boat, and throwing away a lot of potential earnings.

What most of us do it we procrastinate because we don't want to do the things that are not pleasurable to us. Such as working the nights and weekends, but I'm here to tell you, I have never met a successful sales person who didn't work night and weekends. If you know of any please inform me of them, but we all know there isn't any. Go to the most successful person in you company, and I guarantee he or she works nights and weekends.

Now if we have a distant deadline or goal, we procrastinate and this can even affect our heath. Studies have reported that people who procrastinate have a significantly higher stress level and are more likely to have physical illness rather than those who are non-procrastinators.

However, as the deadline approaches, this relationship is reversed; procrastinators report more stress, more symptoms of physical illness, and more medical visits. Since the early 1970's Edward L. Deci and Richard M. Ryan, have conducted research that eventually led to the proposition of the Self Motivational Determination Theory (SDT). This theory focuses on an individual's behaviour to one who is self-motivated and self-determined. SDT identifies three innate needs that, if satisfied, allow optimal function and growth: competence, relatedness, and autonomy. These three are psychological accepts we meed to motivate ourselves to initiate a specific behaviour and mental nutriments that are essential for psychological health and well-being. When our needs are satisfied, there are positive consequences, such as well-being and growth, leading people to be motivated, productive and happiness. When they are thwarted, people's motivation, productivity and happiness plummet

You see a procrastinator focuses less on the future, due to a greater focus on more immediate concerns. A 1992 study showed that "52% of surveyed students indicated that an estimated 80%–95% of college students engage in procrastination, approximately 75% considering themselves procrastinators. Now in any organization we need something to keep us working. Most of the time, the salary or commissions are not enough to keep us working for an organization or company. As sales people we must be motivated to work for the company or organization. If no motivation is present, then our quality of work in general will deteriorate. People differ on a personality dimension called locus of control. This variable refers to individual's beliefs about the location of the factors that control their behavior. At one end of the continuum are high internals who believe that opportunity to control their own behavior rests within themselves. At the other end of the continuum there are high externals who believe that external forces determine their behavior. Now surprisingly, compared with internals, external people see the world as an unpredictable, chancy place in which luck, fate, or powerful people control upon their destinies. There are several reasons why we procrastinate. Now these are some ways we justify procrastination. The first one is HUMOR: making a joke of one's procrastination, that the slapstick or slipshod quality of one's aspirational goal he or she is striving for that's funny. This is a big mistake that we make as sales people funny things are usually negative things so don't be funny of make fun of some who didn't hit their goals. Or we talk about the dog that bit us yesterday or the old man that through a stick at us and told you to get out of his yard. This is only negative information and it can help us in anyway. The next thing that causes us to procrastinate is just plain and simple LAZINESS, because we are too lazy to do our desired task. The next reason is AVIODANCE; this is where we avoid a situation where the task takes place. Example; "oh I can't go out to the field today my tummy hurts". The next reason is DENIAL; this is pretending that procrastinating behavior is not actually procrastinating, but a task which is more important than the avoided one. For example this is where instead of getting more appointments and getting on the phone or on the doors, we say "well I already have 2 appointments already" so we cross of things off things on our clip board and shuffle some papers around and look like we're doing some doing something and again procrastinating the task at hand. The next one is DISTRACTION; we engage or immerse ourselves in other behaviors or actions to prevent awareness of the task. For example playing candy crush on your iPhone instead of making appointments, or cleaning out your presentation kit, (which should have be done in the morning) while there is an appointment waiting now. The last one is VALORISATION, this is pointing out what we achieved in the meantime while we should have been doing something else. Example "we'll I have haven't made any appointments, but I got a good one for next Friday after next". These are all examples on how we justify procrastination. To sum up everything in a nut shell procrastination is the assignation of motivation means, plain and simply that we put of doing the things that make us uncomfortable, the problem with doing so is that if we don't do things now they will pile up until the deadline and most of the time this causes us great stress in the long run. It's a proven fact that higher ratios of successful people are non-procrastinators. When we procrastinate is assonates our motivation, and we are more likely not to hit out goals and achievements. So don't put off until tomorrow, what you can do today. That being said let's get out there make some sales, have some fun and I'll see you at the top

If you have anything you would like to add feel free to Like my Facebook page and post a comment.

David Michael Pena (author)

www.facebook.com/autobiographyofdmp

www.ingramcontent.com/pod-product-compliance
Lightning Source LLC
Chambersburg PA
CBHW051246170526
45165CB00004B/1594